Prayer (
Departed

Christopher Cocksworth

Director of the Southern Theological Education and Training
Scheme (based at Sarum College, Salisbury)

Member of the Church of England Liturgical Commission

GROVE BOOKS LIMITED
RIDLEY HALL RD CAMBRIDGE CB3 9HU

Contents

The Cover Illustration is by Mel Durrant

First Impression August 1997
ISSN 0144-1728
ISBN 1 85174 350 2

1
Introduction

Prayer in relation to the departed has always been a hot potato in the life of the Church of England. It comes out of the oven at moments of liturgical change. Cornish rebels and continental reformers argued over whether the burial rite of the 1549 Prayer Book expressed too little or too much prayer for the departed. In the heat of later liturgical revision the issues were thrashed out at the Savoy Conference in 1661 (as 'Puritans' and 'Anglicans' negotiated over the forthcoming 1662 text), in Parliament in 1927-28 (as members debated the Deposited Prayer Book) and in the House of Laity in 1966-9 (during the debates over Series 1 and 2). Here the Church of England's claim to be both catholic and reformed comes under particular pressure. *Concerned* for catholicity (both in the sense of respecting the traditional practices of the church and recognizing that the church includes all 'in Christ,' the dead as well as the living), and *bound* by its reformed commitment to Scripture and its evangelical confidence in the salvation which God gives, Anglicans have juggled the problem from hand to hand hoping that in the movement between the two a balanced view can be maintained.

We are now in another period of liturgical change. Proposals for a new set of funeral rites are now moving from the private life of the Liturgical Commission to the public life of General Synod. Are the same arguments going to surface? Are the same positions going to be adopted? Is the only option one of compromise which leaves no one fully satisfied? Or are there new ways of looking at the question? Is it possible to avoid some of the old polarities by new perspectives? Can we find a new key so that the godly core of the old songs can be sung to the same tune? This booklet is written in the belief that we can find ways of expressing our prayer in relation to the departed which are faithful to the central concerns of catholicity and to the priorities of evangelical faith. I hope that it may play some small part in identifying these ways. However, I think it is worth giving three warnings about what it to come right from the beginning.

1. It may appear idiosyncratic.

I say *may appear* because although its theological argument simply attempts to recover a very traditional eschatological scheme, I suspect that many will find it hugely naïve, displaying an odd ignorance of all sorts of philosophical questions—particularly in relation to time. Nevertheless, in support of my apparent idiosyncrasies I will draw upon such varied sources as Jürgen Moltmann, Cardinal Ratzinger and the Doctrine Commission of the Church of England, together with some seventeenth century worthies including the *Book of Common Prayer*.

2. It may seem irrelevant.

Because it is focussed on the issue of prayer in relation to the *faithful* departed, I expect some to say that it misses their main worry—that any form of prayer in relation to the dead implies at best that our destiny is open beyond death (rather than decided within the demands of this life and its decisions), and at worst opens the floodgates to doctrines of universalism (which allow for all and sundry to be saved and allow for us to pray for their salvation). These are important and perhaps more pressing pastoral concerns than what we say or do not say about those whose faith was clear for all to see. However, two points can be made in my defence. The first is that these concerns are part of the much wider tension of operating a pastoral system born in Christendom within the ambiguities of an apparently post-Christian nation. The second is that the western liturgical tradition of the Church has never related its prayer for the dead to anyone but those who die *in Christ*. The western church—even at its most un-reformed—has never sought to prise people from the clutches of hell. Purgatory was always in the heavenly realms, not in the nether regions. Nevertheless, although my attention is fixed on prayer in relation to those within the household of faith, it is worth saying at this point that some of these quite proper pastoral and evangelistic concerns can be mitigated by two policies.

i) The first is by the funeral rites clearly articulating the demand as well as the gift of the gospel. The gospel does make firm and sure promises about salvation but it does so within the context of certain expectations. These expectations arise out of the nature of the good news which Christian faith bears. It is *good news* because it speaks of the right ordering of our relationships with God, each other and the whole of creation, structured according to the pattern of God's perfectly ordered life of relationship. The depth of the grace of the gospel is that God invites us into his righteous life of love. The dynamic of this grace therefore assumes some form of response to the invitation. We cannot at the same time speak of salvation in terms of a reconciled set of relationships if we treat the human will to participate in such conditions as of no consequence. The future salvation of which we speak is grounded in the present salvation in which we share as we step into the life of Christ by the enabling of the Spirit. The relational basis of human life requires us to talk of the relational character of Christian salvation which means that the person's relation to God in this life has necessary and decisive consequences for the future life.

4

ii) The second is that funeral rites should be reticent about what they say in relation to the particular person who has died. Any funeral liturgy rests on the belief that the 'judge of all the earth judges justly' (Gen 18.25). Judgment belongs to God and we can leave it to God. Our task is to tell the good news that those who die in Christ will be raised into the glory of God's kingdom. Therefore any praying which we do in relation to the departed—even our prayer of thanks for God's assurance of salvation—is generally better done in the plural rather than the singular. This way we can state the gospel promises for God's people without preempting God's judgment of a particular person (1 Cor 5.10).

3. It probably looks unsound.

I am conscious that although I consider myself to be writing as an evangelical, some of what I say may not be immediately pleasing to evangelical ears. All I can say is that I have found my views on these matters shifting as I have grappled with Scripture—and especially with its view of the eschatological fullness of salvation. In the fashion of Grove booklets, I do not claim that my reading of Scripture is the last word on the subject but at least it is a word which has arisen from a genuine engagement with biblical perspectives. I am quite happy for my views to go on shifting as scriptural truth becomes clearer to me and so I await further clarification from those who might read different views from the biblical material.

However, before we begin to swim in the theological waters we need to wet our feet in some of the streams of history.

2
Looking at History

The Reformation

There is no doubt that the church which the Reformers wanted to reform did all sorts of things in its popular piety, said all sort of things in its public liturgy and believed all sort of things in its official places which were deeply damaging to the promises of salvation found in the pages of the Bible. Indeed, Tetzel's sale of indulgences to speed people through the pain of purgatory (and to paint St Peter's Church in Rome) was the flint that sparked the Reformation, as it struck against the rock of grace uncovered by Luther, buried beneath the sand of merit. As the fire spread to England, Cranmer set about recasting the liturgy. His initial aim (as expressed in his 1549 burial rite) seems to have been to excise any implication of a purgatorial process in which the sins of the dead are assuaged by the prayers of the living. It was not to remove prayer for the departed *per se*. Thus his 1549 burial rite prays:

> Grant unto this thy servant...that he...may dwell in the region of light, with Abraham, Isaac, and Jacob, the place where there is no weeping, sorrow or heaviness: and when that dreadful day of the general resurrection shall come, make him to rise also with the just and righteous, and receive this body again to glory.

Cranmer's subsequent aim (as shown in his 1552 rite) seems to have been to express a confident assurance that those who die in Christ are safe with him. However, although this involved removing any petition for the dead to be welcomed into Christ's presence, including a specific commendation of the soul to God, it did not require all prayerful mention of the departed to be excised. A strong sense of thanksgiving could and should be quite properly expressed. But Cranmer also felt that it was permissible to relate the person who was being buried to the congregation which was doing the burying in a prayer for their mutual experience of God's kingdom:

> We give thee hearty thanks...beseeching thee that it may please thee of thy gracious goodness, shortly to accomplish the number of thine elect, and to hasten thy kingdom, that we with this our brother, and all other departed in the true faith of thy holy name, may have our perfect consummation and bliss, both in body and soul, in thy eternal and everlasting glory.

Here, as in the 1549 rite, the phrase 'we with him' does not refer to our share in that which the dead already have.[1] Rather, it looks forward to our common share in that which is to come—the resurrection of the dead and the fullness of life with God. It is interesting that in 1662 the petition is softened by removing the direct reference to the particular person who has died and making it into a more general association of all the living and all the dead in Christ:

> ...beseeching thee...to hasten thy kingdom, that we with all those that are departed...

However, 1552 and 1662 are agreed in their avoidance of any implication that God's acceptance of those who have died in Christ into his eschatological kingdom is still an open question, even less one that can be affected by our prayers. Rather than praying that 'this our brother...may be found acceptable in thy sight,' as 1549 does at one point, they both simply ask that that which God has promised for his faithful people will be soon fulfilled.

When we turn to the communion rite we can see a similar but slightly more complex picture. In his 1549 intercessions Cranmer retains prayer for the faithful departed in much the same way as in the burial rite—praying for mercy and peace for those who rest in Christ and for acceptance at Christ's right hand for all who await the resurrection. In 1552 Cranmer took out any reference to the dead and made it clear that the prayer is for 'Christ's Church *militant here on earth.*' The 1662 revisers kept the delineation of the prayer to the living but reintroduced a commemoration of the departed, giving thanks for them and 'beseeching' God to

> give us grace so to follow their good examples, that with them we may be partakers of thy heavenly kingdom.

I have always accepted the standard interpretation of evangelical *Prayer Book* apologetics that this simply asks that we may enter into the bliss which the dead now enjoy. But in the light of recent study, such as the foregoing analysis of the burial rite, I am not so sure that this is right. The sixteenth and seventeenth centuries were much more faithful to the biblical pattern of death–sleep–resurrection than we have become. It seems possible to me that the 1662 petition includes the dead with the living in a prayer for that which

---

1 See the 1549 Collect: 'We meekly beseech thee (O Father) to raise us from the death of sin, unto the life of righteousness, that when we shall depart this life, we may sleep in [Christ] (as our hope is this our brother doeth) and at the general resurrection in the last day, both we and this our brother departed, receiving again our bodies, and rising again in thy most gracious favour: may with all thine elect Saints, obtain eternal joy.'

we all await—the coming of the fullness of the kingdom in the new creation. It is interesting that Charles Wheatly also found himself in somewhat of a quandary over this petition. Wheatly's *Rational Illustration of the Book of Common Prayer* was first published in 1710 and became the standard commentary on the Prayer Book until well into the nineteenth century. He recognized that the restriction of the intercession to the 'Church on earth' suggests that the 1662 revisers were not seeking to pray for the dead as well as the living. On the other hand, given the eschatological framework with which the writers were working, he felt that the inclusion of the dead in the prayer is at least implied by the phrase 'with them we.' Wheatly claimed that despite differences over eschatological details, the leaders of the 'primitive Church' were agreed that the 'interval between death and the end of the world is a state of expectation and imperfect bliss, in which the souls of the righteous wait for the completion and perfection of their happiness at the consummation of all things.' He believed that this scheme allowed for prayer that we 'might all together attain a blessed and glorious resurrection, and be brought at last to a perfect fruition of happiness in heaven.'[2]

The Deposited Prayer Book

Prayer in relation to the dead was one of the many controversial areas in *The Deposited Prayer Book* presented to Parliament in 1927. In general the proposed Prayer Book added to the 1662 material in an attempt to make the authorized liturgy more attractive to the catholic constituency. For our purposes four additions should be noted. First, 'The Commemoration of All Souls' was reintroduced to the Calendar in addition to All Saints' Day. Second, a commendation of the faithful departed was returned to the intercessions in the communion rite (following 1549) together with a commemoration of the saints. Third, (again following 1549) the burial rite included a commendation of the soul as well as the committal of the body and prayed that the deceased 'may be found acceptable' in God's sight at the judgment (though unlike 1549 it did not refer in this prayer to the resurrection). The burial service also introduced a prayer 'for those we love, but see no longer,' asking God to 'let light perpetual shine upon them' and 'work in them the good purpose of thy perfect will.'[3]

Two historical comments and one theological comment need to be made on these proposals. Historically, they should be seen not only against the

---

2   Charles Wheatly. *A Rational Illustration of the Book of Common Prayer of the Church of England* (London: Henry Bohn. 1852) pp 282-284 (p 282).
3   The Prayer Book also proposed two traditional formulae for commending the departed:
     'Rest eternal grant unto them. O Lord: and let light perpetual shine upon them' (in the burial service).
     'May the souls of the departed. through the mercy of God. rest in peace' (in the service of Prime).

backdrop of the catholic revival in the Church of England but also against the memory of the appalling casualties of the first world war. The devastation of the war left vast quantities of people searching for some way to voice their love and concern for those they lost on the fields of battle, and led many either to the fuller rites of the Roman Church or to the strange but enticing promises of the medium. Although the proposals were rejected by Parliament they have had a lasting effect upon the Church. Much of its material was included in *The Shorter Prayer Book* issued by the Archbishops in 1948. The 1928 'Order for the Burial of the Dead' became particularly popular and was finally authorized—though not without a fight—in 1966 in the form of Series 1.

Theologically, the most serious fault of the material was that it dismembered the eschatological framework of the *Prayer Book*. This is most evident in its 'Prayer for the whole state of Christ's Church.' Clearly the change in title signifies a strong desire to include the departed in the prayer. In itself this need not have been objectionable. We have seen that 1662 was confused at this point. Clarification could have been helpful. However, the way the prayer went about praying in relation to the departed introduced two problems. First, it legitimized the spurious distinction which lay behind its inclusion of 'All Soul's Day,' that the general mass of the faithful departed can be distinguished in terms of their present experience of salvation from the 'Saints, who have been lights of the world in their generations.' Second and consequently, when it prayed that 'we may be partakers with them of thy heavenly kingdom' it assumed that the saints are already there. This negates the biblical scheme which the sixteenth and seventeenth century Prayer Books—including 1549—carefully recovered: that all the faithful are waiting for the resurrection which will bring the completion of salvation. The commendation of the departed in *The Deposited Prayer Book* became detached from the anticipation of the entry of all God's people into the fullness of the kingdom. It sat as an isolated petition which can only be made sense of by the medieval pattern in which death is followed by a purgatorial process leading to an eventual sainthood.

Towards the ASB

The next attempt at liturgical revision aimed to provide an alternative to rather than a replacement of the 1662 *Prayer Book*. The first stab at an alternative set of services began to see the light of day in the early 1960s. They were bound together in a volume called *Alternative Services: Second Series*[4] which the Archbishops recommended for introduction at the Convocations and

---

4   The Church of England Liturgical Commission, *Alternative Services: Second Series* (London: SPCK, 1965).

House of Laity. 'The Draft Order for Holy Communion' included an optional petition over which the whole service was later to stumble:

> Remember those who have died in faith, and sleep in the peace of Christ, and grant them a share in thy eternal kingdom.

When a slightly reworked Draft Order was published it included a note of dissent by Colin Buchanan, the Liturgical Commission's newest member. The main focus of his dissent was the oblation of the bread and cup in the eucharistic prayer but he also objected to the petition for the departed. He was constructively supported by the House of Laity which not only shared some of his reservations about the text but produced a compromise which later won the day:

> Hear us as we remember those who have died in faith and grant us with them a share in thy eternal kingdom.

By the standards of 1927/8 the original form of the petition had much in its favour. It retained a biblical eschatology of sleep followed by resurrection. But its imperatives of 'remember' and 'grant,' together with its reference to the dead in isolation from the living meant that it was a long way from what evangelicals, with memories of the former battles still alive, could accept. The disadvantage of the compromise text was that it flattened the eschatology of the original and implied that the faithful departed enjoy now 'the eternal kingdom,' leaving us to pray only that we might join them there. I imagine this is why it was acceptable to evangelicals.

Although the Second Series' proposals for the burial rite began with a smoother passage, they were eventually sunk without much trace by the House of Laity. Their eschatology was much more confused than the original petition for the departed in the communion rite. Reference to the future resurrection of believers seems to have been studiously avoided leaving the mandatory commendation and the optional prayers for the departed lacking an undergirding theological rationale.[5]

Following the difficulties faced over prayers for the departed, the Doctrine Commission was asked to produce a report on the subject. The carefully argued Report which was published in 1971 came to the conclusion that the eschatological framework of the New Testament allows us to pray for the faithful departed in this way:

---

5 For example, the Collect: 'Raise us, we beseech thee, from the death of sin unto the life of righteousness; that *when we shall depart this life* we may with this our brother be found acceptable unto thee...' (My emphasis)

May God in his infinite love and mercy bring the whole Church, living and departed in the Lord Jesus, to a joyful resurrection and the fulfilment of his eternal kingdom.[6]

The prayer found its way into the Series 3 funeral rite and then, along with most of the Series 3 service, into the *ASB*. Although there might be better ways of expressing what it says, the prayer represents an important and underestimated contribution to the liturgical perplexities which the Church of England has experienced over the issue of prayer in relation to the departed. Nevertheless, I fear that its potential to help us to avoid muddles in the next stage of discussions, debates and decisions about the new proposals will not be maximized unless its theological reasoning can be clarified. It is to this task that I now turn by focusing on the significance of the resurrection of the body in Christian eschatology.

---

6   *Prayer and the Departed: A Report of the Archbishops' Commission on Christian Doctrine* (London: SPCK, 1971) p 51. For the view of an earlier report on Christian Doctrine about prayer and the departed see, *Doctrine and the Church of England: The Report of the Commission on Christian Doctrine Appointed in 1922* (London: SPCK, 1938) pp 214-216.

3
Recovering a Biblical Eschatology

As I have already said, the underlying eschatological pattern of the New Testament is of death–sleep–resurrection (for example, 1 Thess 4.13-18; 1 Cor 15.51-52). Even John's tendency towards realized eschatology stops short of conflating the linear scheme; Christ will raise us up at the last day (John 6.54). We have seen that the basic pattern is reflected in the *Prayer Book* Burial Service which talks of believers resting in Christ until 'the general resurrection of the last day' (Collect). I suspect that the impasse between catholics and evangelicals in the Church of England over prayer and the departed is caused in part by a departure from this scheme and, accordingly, by a failure to take the New Testament's teaching on the resurrection with full seriousness. Before exploring this scheme more fully it is worth noting something of what the resurrection means for our understanding of humanity.

The resurrection tells us that a person is a psychosomatic being. Human life is an embodied existence. The narratives of Jesus' resurrection and Paul's teaching on the meaning of the resurrection make it clear that Jesus' new humanity intrinsically includes a bodily dimension.

The resurrection tells us that a person is a social being. Human life is lived out in a network of interdependent relationships. The body is the means by which human beings express themselves and relate to each other. The biblical images of resurrection refer to a corporate experience of salvation in which the salvation of the one is dependent on the salvation of the other.

The resurrection tells us that a person is a material being. Human life is bound to the material order of creation. This of course does not mean that we are tied to the exact material of our present existence but rather that we are inextricably part of the creation which is waiting for its renewal and transformation into the glory which God intends. This is why the whole creation 'waits in eager longing' for the revelation of our true existence as God's children when our bodies will be redeemed (Rom 8.19-23; 2 Cor 5.2-5).

The doctrine of the resurrection of the dead first came to expression during and after the Jewish exile when the prophets looked forward to the revelation of YHWH's lordship over all things. They prophesied that YHWH's universal reign would be demonstrated in his renewal of creation to the point at which it would become a place fit for him to dwell. The implication of this is that God has covenanted himself to the temporal and spatial outworking of his purposes. God has set himself a task to do with our creation: to bring it to glory. In the language of Jewish eschatology cast in the grammar of Pauline Christology, this will not be complete until every ruler, authority

12

and power, including the last enemy of death, is subjected to the life giving rule of Christ, and the Son hands over the kingdom which he has won to the Father (1 Cor 15.24).[7]

However, the pattern of death–sleep–resurrection is a problematic one even as far as the New Testament is concerned. It raises the question of what is meant by the 'sleep' or 'rest.' I can discern three interpretations in the tradition of the church.

Conscious Intermediate State

The first is that the 'sleep' is a conscious intermediate state between death and resurrection. A number of Jewish motifs picturing such a state can be found in the New Testament. Jewish ideas of the dead being alive in paradise, sometimes described as 'the bosom of Abraham,' can be found in Luke (16.19-31; 23.42-3). Scenes of the souls of the departed living within the altar of God current in Jewish apocalyptic imagery appear in the book of Revelation (6.9). From a more distinctively Christian perspective Paul talks confidently of being 'at home with the Lord' and 'away from the body' (2 Cor 5.6-7). Elsewhere he speaks movingly about dying and being 'with the Lord' (Phil 1.21-23) within the framework of the future *parousia* and resurrection of the body (Phil 3.19-20).

Understandings of the intermediate state developed further as time moved on. In general terms the Eastern tradition spoke of an ongoing process of glorification, while the West, from as early as Tertullian in the late second century, focussed on a process of purification (later articulated in the doctrine of purgatory). A significant stage in the Western development took place in 1336 when Benedict XII published his *Benedictus Deus*. The Bull declared that those souls who are in no need of further purification can leave, or in some cases, bypass the intermediate state and enter the heavenly bliss. This (unnecessary) complication of the simple scheme of death–'rest in Christ' (presence with Christ)–resurrection implies three departures from the New Testament understanding of salvation. First, eschatological salvation is individualized. *My* experience of salvation is dependent only on *my* sanctification and ceases to be interdependent with the salvation of *others*. Second, the resurrection of the body and therefore the renewal of creation is downgraded. Yes, the Bull concedes that the resurrection is still to come but it reduces it to a formality. It no longer belongs to the heart of Christian eschatology as the transfiguration of God's world into the glorious liberty for which it was first fashioned. Third, prayer for the salvation of particular individuals beyond death is almost necessitated. Because each individual soul is on a journey

---

7 'In the primitive Christian expectation, the future of the individual man is completely dependent upon the future of the entire redemptive history.' Oscar Cullman, *Christ and Time* (London: SCM, 1962) p 231.

through purgatory to heaven, rather than simply with Christ waiting for the fullness of salvation, the case for prayer to aid that journey becomes irresistible.

Unconscious Intermediate State

A second interpretation of the 'sleep' is that it is an unconscious intermediate state. This understanding seems to be implied by certain Pauline writings. For example in 1 Thess 4.13-17 those who have 'fallen asleep' are awoken by the Lord's command at the *parousia*. Luther seems to adopt this perspective on death. However, he argued that as far as the individual's perception is concerned, the resurrection happens almost instantaneously with death:

> Just as at night one hears the clock strike and know not how long we have slept, so too, and how much more, are in death a thousand years soon past. Before a man should turn around, he is already a fair angel...[8]

In his poem 'Dooms-Day' George Herbert also pictures death as an unconscious, dreamless sleep from which we will arise on the Day of the Lord:

> Come Away.
> Make no delay.
> Summon all the dust to rise,
> Till it stirred, and rubbed the eyes;
> While this member jogs the other,
> Each whispering, *Live you brother?*[9]

The merit of this interpretation of the sleep is that it refuses to disrupt the unity of psychosomatic existence. Whereas the Church's tradition, following, as we have seen, Jewish tradition, appealed to the story of Lazarus in the bosom of Abraham as an example of a body-soul distinction, Luther insisted:

> *Totus Abraham:* the whole man shall live! What you do is to tear me off a bit of Abraham and say, 'This is what shall live'...A soul which is in heaven and desires the body: it must be a crazy soul we are talking about.[10]

---

8 *W A* 36. 548. It appears that The Doctrine Commission's Report, *The Mystery of Salvation* (London: CHP, 1995), takes a similar view: 'Because the "time" of the new creation is a new time, it need bear no simple or sequential relationship to the time we presently experience. Though we die at different times, we may all enter into our destiny together' (p 196). I take this to refer to the consciousness of salvation rather than to imply the de-historicization of salvation.

9 From *The Temple*.

10 *W A* 2. 219

One of my children recently expressed a similar view around the tea table. Responding to one of his brothers who said that our spirits go to heaven when we die, my nine year old said, 'But how can you *see* yourself if you are a spirit? How can you *be* yourself if you are a spirit?' Like Luther he could not conceive of human existence in abstraction from the embodiment which defines, shapes and directs our individuality.

Nevertheless, although a conscious bodiless state creates obvious anthropological complexities, the concept of an unconscious intermediate state is also not without its difficulties. To say that a person is 'asleep in Christ' presupposes a continuing existence of the self between the end of the natural body and the beginning of the resurrection body. What is maintained in existence and how can it be the authentic reality of the person if his or her bodily dimension has ceased to be?[11]

No intermediate state

A third understanding of the 'sleep' is that it is simply a mythological picture drawn from the temporal perspective of our human eyes. In reality the dead have been raised already to newness of life. They have stepped out of our time into the eternity of God where all God's promises are fulfilled in one eternal moment. This view of resurrection *in* death is prevalent in much modern Roman Catholic theology which, in turn, is indebted to the eschatology of the early Barth. It is also the mind-set of evangelical piety and largely explains why evangelicals find prayer for the dead such an extraordinary practice. How can we pray for those in whom God's purposes of salvation have been fulfilled? To pray for those who are now experiencing the completion of their eschatological salvation seems utterly unnecessary and also dangerously destructive to our sense of the assurance of salvation.

In 1979 The Congregation for the Defence of the Faith published a 'Letter on Certain Questions of Eschatology' in an attempt to counteract and correct the emerging consensus in favour of resurrection *in* death. Interestingly, a central plank in the Congregation's argument was that if the faithful have already undergone their resurrection, the church's practice of intercession for the dead is rendered meaningless. There is no point in praying for those who have everything.[12]

---

11 *The Mystery of Salvation* defines language about the soul in terms of 'the information-bearing pattern' of the person. The embodiment of the pattern is dissolved at death 'but the person whose that pattern is, is "remembered" by God, who in love holds that unique being in his care' (p 191).

12 For a discussion of the document see, 'Appendix' in Johann Auer and Joseph Ratzinger, *Dogmatic Theology: Eschatology, Death and Eternal Life* (Washington: Catholic University of America Press, 1988 [ET]) pp 241-60. Throughout the book Ratzinger argues powerfully and carefully *against* resurrection in death and *for* the traditional framework of Christian eschatology: 'The thesis of resurrection in death dematerializes the resurrection. It entails that real matter has no part in the event of the consummation. This theory reduces

Moltmann also argues against the idea of resurrection *in* death on the grounds that it dissolves 'our bodily solidarity with this earth':

But is not every grave in this earth a sign that human beings and the earth belong together, and will only be redeemed together? Without 'the new earth' there is no 'resurrection of the body.'[13]

Moltmann insists that our eschatology must be rooted in the Christ who is himself *'on the way* to God's kingdom.'[14] Christ's lordship is not yet demonstrated over all things. That is why we still pray for the coming of God's kingdom. The Spirit still yearns for the renewal of creation and calls upon Christ to manifest the new heaven and new earth. (Rom 8.22-7; Rev 22.20). That is why our prayer is not simply thanksgiving for the salvation that has come but is impassioned intercession for the salvation which is still to come. The book of Revelation gives us a hint that the dead in Christ yearn also for this kingdom to come as they cry 'Sovereign Lord...How long will it be before you judge...the earth?' (6.10).

In terms of the piety in which I was formed I now find myself dissatisfied with the assumption that the faithful dead are experiencing the fullness of salvation because it isolates an individual's salvation from the salvation of others and abstracts the salvation of humanity from the salvation of the world. Furthermore it mythologizes the great scheme of salvation (which works from God's creation of the world to its new creation) by putting in its place an eternal dimension which is the true sphere of salvation. We are left to assume that God is not really committed to perfecting that which he has made but rather to plucking it out from this world into an eternal realm where all is as it should be. Accordingly the *parousia*, the judgment and general resurrection are reduced simply to pictures of existential encounter. They are no longer markers of God's covenant with our space and time.[15]

Christian hope to the level of the individual. If individual men and women *qua* individuals can, through death, enter upon the End, then history as such remains outside salvation and cannot receive its own fulfilment' (p 267).

For a similar expression from a very different source, note: 'The soul is not saved if the body does not rise, since this would mean that God had abandoned the work of his hands. Then all the promises would collapse.' Adrio König, *The Eclipse of Christ in Eschatology* (London, Marshall, Morgan and Scott, 1989 [ET]) p 226.

13 *The Coming of God: Christian Eschatology* (London, SCM, 1996 [ET]) p 104.

14 *The Coming of God*, p 104.

15 The same concerns are strongly expressed in *The Mystery of Salvation:* 'The world of space and time, along with the material world, are reclaimed in the resurrection of Jesus, and are to be fulfilled in the resurrection of Jesus' people and the consequent transformation of the whole cosmos (Rom 8.18-27)' (p 82).

Conclusions

If, contrary to the third view, we retain the traditional eschatological pattern of death—'sleep'—resurrection, what can we say about prayer in relation to the faithful departed? I suggest three principles.

First, we must not undermine a sense of assurance that God will fulfil his promises of salvation for all who have died in Christ. Death cannot separate us from the love God has for us in Christ. This love has been poured into our hearts by the Holy Spirit who remains an unmovable guarantee of our future (2 Cor 5.5). If the power which raised Christ from the dead is at work in people when alive (Eph 1.17-20), it will not cease when they die. There is no need to fear for the faithful. They are bearers of God's life-giving Spirit. They have been baptized into the life of God's Son. Their presence with Christ and their future in his kingdom are secure.

Second, we must express our confidence that the faithful departed are 'in Christ.' Although the public prayer of the Church's liturgy will remain agnostic about how the dead experience being 'in Christ,' it should affirm that they continue in relationship with him and that we continue in relationship with them. Christ is the Lord of the living and the dead. Paul assured his Thessalonian readers, who were grieving over the death of some of their number, that 'whether awake or asleep' we 'live with the Lord' (1 Thess 5.9-10).[16]

Third, we must retain a recognition that the fullness of salvation is still to come for the dead as well as the living.[17] The Spirit by whom they have been

16 I find myself inclined to the view that the biblical notion of 'sleep' refers to a conscious enjoyment of life with Christ within an alternative condition of space and time. Four factors point me in this direction. First, it is difficult to make sense of a fellowship or common life with Christ which does not involve consciousness. Second, the traditional chronology of Jesus' dying and rising supports a case for activity between death and resurrection. Between commending his spirit to the Father at his death and rising on the third day, Jesus stands in conscious solidarity with the dead and ministers to them. Third, the pictures of the heavenly places in the Book of Revelation, painted with the brush strokes of Jewish apocalyptic, tell of a rich life of praise in the presence of Christ. But the heavenly life is not an insulated celestial existence. It is a life structured around the war which Christ is waging to implement his victory and usher in the new creation. Fourth, the Pauline emphasis on 'being with the Lord' is too strong to indicate anything less than a conscious enjoyment of his presence.
17 To support the view that the fullness of God's purposes for the dead lies in the future, I quote from a number of sources beginning with the modern and ending with the ancient.
'Before God, the living and the dead are in the same situation. The dead are not lost, but they are not finally saved either...The common hope for the future of eternal life and the new creation binds us together. It is true that "it has not yet appeared" what we—and they—will be, but when he appears we—and they—will see him as he is and be like him (1 John 3.2).' Moltmann, *Coming of God* (1996) pp 106-7.
'But...all will agree that there remains a fuller realization of God's purpose for us all at the end' *Mystery of Salvation* (1995) p 191.
'Hence, *the dead likewise live in a condition in which the tension between present and future still exists,*' Cullman, *Christ and Time* (1962) p 240.
'Consider how near we must be to each other, when the dead are said to be imperfect without us...All are imperfect until Christ shall come. Even the best are so, till the Resurrection.' John Keble (1792-1866), 'Fellowship in the Saints' in *Outlines of Instructions*

baptized into Christ remains the eschatological Spirit whose work is to manifest the victory of Christ in the heavens and the earth. He is the earnest as well as the guarantee of their place in the coming kingdom (2 Cor 5.5). Even if we claim that whether in an unconscious or conscious intermediate state the dead step into a different experience of time, we must not imply that their time and history will not once again intersect with our time and history. If we do so we fall into the problems identified in the third view and we make God's redemptive plan redundant. God is committed to renewing the face of the earth by the Spirit whose sighs can be heard in its pain. Neither must we forget that our prayer is always from the perspective of our time. We cannot step out of our time continuum.[18] The same reason why we do not pray for things which have already happened applies to why we continue to pray for things which have not happened. To attempt to do otherwise is to negate a dimension of human existence to which we are bound. It is like pretending that we are not bound by space and can be in several places at the same time.

Each time we pray for the coming of the kingdom we are praying for the dead as well as the living to enter into the completion of God's purposes. Christ has not yet fulfilled his promise to raise them up at the last day (John 6.54). This work remains part of his prayer and part of the Spirit's yearning. By the power of the Spirit and in union with Christ we pray that God will demonstrate Christ's victory over all things, including the last enemy of death,

---

or Meditations by John Keble, edited by R F Wilson (Oxford: University Press, 1860) p 291.
'Though their souls be always in an estate of blessedness, yet they want the consummation of this blessedness, extensively at least, until the body be reunited with the soul; and (as it is piously and probably believed) intensively also,—that the soul hath not yet so full and clear a vision of God, as it shall have hereafter.' John Bramhall (1594-1663), 'The Answer to La Milletiére' in Works (LACT, 1842) pp 59f.
'For the apostles too have not received their joy: they likewise are waiting for me to participate in their joy. So it is that the saints who depart from here do not immediately receive the full reward of their merits, but wait for us, even if we delay, even if we remain sluggish...Do you see, then? Abraham is still waiting to attain perfection. Isaac and Jacob and all the prophets are waiting for us in order to attain the perfect blessedness together with us. This is the reason why judgment is kept a secret, being postponed until the Last Day. It is "one body" which is waiting for justification, "one body" which rises for judgment. "Though there are many members, yet there is only one body. The eye cannot say to the hand, I do not need you." Even if the eye is sound and fit for seeing, if the other members were lacking, what would the joy of the eye be? You will have joy when you depart this life if you are a saint. But your joy will be complete only when no member of your body is lacking to you. For you will wait, just as you are awaited.' Origen (c185-c254), 'Sermon on Leviticus 7.1-2,' quoted by Ratzinger in Eschatology, p 186.
18 I say this because it might be argued that if the dead do not experience time (as we know it) but simply enter the resurrection in their next conscious moment, there is no need to pray for their resurrection because from their perspective it has already happened, there being no time delay in their experience. But their perspective is not ours. We can only pray within the conditions of our perspective. Indeed, I want to go further and say that even if the dead have a very different measurement of time from the living (which seems reasonable to suppose), the resurrection of the dead still has not happened. It remains in the future. To say otherwise is to say that it is not this world which is redeemed.

by raising all those who belong to Christ into the imperishable life of the new creation (1 Cor 15.20-28, 50-57; 2 Cor 5.2-4). This does not mean that we doubt whether Christ will complete his purposes for the dead any more than we doubt whether he will do so for the living. It means only that our prayer for the coming of this kingdom which lies at the centre of our living as Christians embraces everything that waits in longing for the kingdom's coming.

Inevitably at the time of death all these expressions of prayer in relation to the departed will revolve around a particular individual. However, as time proceeds beyond the period of mourning, the focus should properly shift from the one (who has died) to the many (faithful departed) in whom that person is in relationship and with whom, together with the whole of creation, we are bound in a common hope.

4

Considering Practice

We must now consider what the principles identified at the end of the last chapter mean for our practice. But before looking at particular texts we need to explore some aspects of the funeral's pastoral function.

An important part of the ministry surrounding the funeral is to enable the family and friends of the deceased to face the reality of death within the hope forged in human history through the death and resurrection of Jesus Christ and within the comfort and strength of the Holy Spirit.

Facing the reality of death is a long business. It is like being on a journey. The horizon is always changing, not because it has changed but because we have moved and so see things differently. All sorts of voices, from social anthropologists and bereavement counsellors, to the kindly person who has been there before and whispers to us in our grief 'it will take time,' tell us that handling the death of a loved one is a long process with many stages along the way. Good anthropology (a proper understanding of human life) and good liturgy (a proper understanding of the words and rituals supporting human life) are closely connected. Providing that the anthropology is rooted in good theology (a proper understanding of the divine life, in which image we are made), liturgy should be to anthropology what a road is to a car—a carefully constructed surface for the vehicle's journey.

The closest the *BCP* comes to providing liturgical support (in addition to the funeral itself) for the process of bereavement is in its rite of 'Visitation of the Sick.' As well as ministering to the person who is ill—and assumed to be dying—this provision gives the family and friends an opportunity to prepare for the death. The *ASB* goes slightly further by providing 'A Service which may be used before a Funeral' and by introducing a 'Commemoration of the Faithful Departed' into the Calendar.[19] *The Promise of His Glory* (*POHG*) gives additional and in some cases contentious material for the latter, including a version of the Orthodox Kontakion (Give rest, O Christ, to your servants with your saints) and a version of the prayer which is popular in other parts of the Anglican Communion (Acknowledge, we pray, the sheep of your fold). More recent funeral rites have shown much more effort to key into the various stages along the way by a range of provisions from the time of death to later anniversaries. The leader in the field has been the Roman Catholic *Order of Christian Funerals*,[20] its staged approach to the funeral rite clearly being a

---

19 Its omission of an equivalent to the Visitation of the Sick was corrected with the publication of *Ministry to the Sick* in 1983 and *Ministry at the Time of Death* in 1991.
20 (London: Geoffrey Chapman, 1991).

major source of inspiration for the present proposals in the Church of England.

The staged approach is to be welcomed for at least two reasons. First, people need to be ministered to in different ways at different stages of their bereavement process. Second, we need to pray in different ways at different points of proximity to the death. I have found myself wanting to pray in one way at or near the moment of death—including the moment I hear of the death—and in quite another way at a memorial service six months after the death. I remember a moving scene in *Shadowlands*, the film about C S Lewis. Lewis is at his wife's bedside watching her die. After she breathes her last he cries out through his tears, 'Sweet Jesus, hold her tight.' Can we say anything less at these times? I also remember *Thought for the Day* on the morning after John Smith's tragic death. With the nation in a state of shock at the loss of the person many expected to be the next Prime Minister, Philip Crowe spoke sensitively about his life and faith and prayed, 'May he rest in peace and rise in glory.' My heart echoed the prayer. On another occasion my family heard the news of the sudden death of a strong and good woman we had known in another parish. We turned to the *Pocket Version of Celebrating Common Prayer* and used the simple order of Commendation. It seemed the natural thing to do.

All these prayers involved an element of intercession for the person to be received by Christ. Were they therefore contrary to my first two principles? Do such prayers undermine both our assurance that God will fulfil his purposes of salvation for all who have died in Christ and our confidence that the faithful departed are 'in Christ,' 'with the Lord'? I do not think they do, providing they are rooted in the moment of death—any more than Jesus' commendation of his spirit to the Father implied a lack of assurance and confidence that God would receive him and raise him up on the third day. These are prayers of 'handing over.' They articulate a transfer or exchange. We are not saying to God 'we doubt your willingness to do this and feel that you need some encouragement from us to cooperate.' In fact, we are saying the opposite: 'We know that you are ready to do this and we entrust that for which we have had some responsibility into your hands so that you can take your full responsibility.' We are saying no more than 'do as you have promised.'

However, the more such prayers become distanced from the moment of death, the more they sound like anxious imprecations rather than natural, almost unavoidable, commendations. This is why I would find it odd to pray at a Commemoration of the Faithful Departed, as invited to in *POHG*, 'Acknowledge, we pray, the sheep of your fold.' Assuming that we are commemorating those who have been dead for some time, I can make little sense of asking Christ to acknowledge those we have already commended into God's keeping. It either involves asking Christ to do what he has already done or implies that God has not kept his promises.

The more difficult questions come when trying to determine which way of praying is appropriate for a funeral service. Interestingly, Jewish culture regards the funeral as a forty-day process. Clearly, the time of death is concentrated in a moment and the bereavement is elongated over years, but the Jewish practice is a good reminder that the *rites* associated with death span an intermediate period, neither completed in the immediate nor extending indefinitely. The actual funeral service is sometimes described as a ritualization of the moment of death. Both for those who may have been present at the death but numbed by its immediate trauma and for those who were not able to be at the bedside or who did not hear about it until sometime later, the funeral acts as the public, corporate and focused ritual rehearsal of the handing over to God.

Most will agree that the funeral should involve entrusting or commending the person into the hands of God, even though many at the service will have done so privately at different times and places. There will be more disagreement over what level of intercession should accompany the commendation. A case can be made for saying that whatever is permissible at the moment of death should be allowed in its ritualization at the funeral. On the other hand, because the funeral is both a social and public event and necessarily somewhat distanced from the immediate impact of death, I do not think we can treat it simply as an equivalent to the moment of death. Its ritual identity gives it a certain form which distinguishes it from a private response to the news of a death.

A major question to be faced in the debates over the new proposals is whether the following two texts are appropriate commendations for the funeral service:

Go forth from this world:
in the love of God the Father
who created you,
in the mercy of Jesus Christ
who redeemed you,
in the power of the Holy Spirit
who strengthens you.
May the heavenly host sustain you
and the company of heaven enfold you.
In communion with all the faithful,
may you dwell this day in peace.

Into your hands O merciful Saviour,
we commend your servant *N.*
Acknowledge, we pray, a sheep of your own fold,
a lamb of your own flock,

a sinner of your own redeeming.
Enfold *him/her* in your arms of mercy,
in the blessed rest of everlasting peace,
and in the glorious company of all the saints in light.

Some will find these quite justifiable as texts to be used in the immediate orbit of death but unacceptable in the later setting of a funeral.[21] My problem with them is not so much the awkwardness of transposing texts which naturally belong to the vicinity of *dying* to a later context where they fit less well, but rather the absence of a reference to the resurrection and future glory in them. The second prayer could be made more serviceable by softening its commendatory element and strengthening its eschatological aspect:

Into your hands O merciful Saviour,
we commend your servant N.
Receive, we pray, a sheep of your own fold,
a lamb of your own flock,
a sinner of your own redeeming.
Enfold *him/her* in your arms of mercy,
in the blessed fellowship of your peace,
in the joyful company of all the saints;
and at the coming of Christ raise *him/her* into the eternal glory of your
    unshakable kingdom
where all things are made new.[22]

However, there are problems with changing well-known texts. My guess is that it is better to use new texts based on agreed principles.

At other points, however, the new proposals work with a sound eschatological framework which allows the liturgy to express a sense of the living

21 The form of the first prayer ('Go forth') as an *address to the person* proves that it belongs to the ministry surrounding the moment of death. In *Ministry at the Time of Death* it is spoken to the dying rather than the dead person. Of course it is quite possible that the person may have died before these word are said but the line separating life from death in the last moments of someone's life is very thin. Even if the person is medically dead it is still natural for us to go on saying our final farewells and words of love. But the further we move from the death the more questionable it becomes to speak directly to the dead.

22 I could be persuaded to pray the last six lines of this revised prayer (possibly with the change of 'enfold' to 'hold') beyond the funeral rites. In other words, although I have never felt the need in practice, I am prepared in principle to pray that the dead will continue to *rest in peace* as well as to *rise in glory*. This is not because I doubt whether they are 'with the Lord' but because I recognize that until Christ has established his kingdom throughout the cosmos and handed it to his Father (1 Cor 15.24-28), the living and the dead are bound by, as Moltmann puts it 'a common danger' *(Coming of God,* p 106) as well as a common hope. The purposes of God for all that he has made will not be complete until that day and so there is still room for prayer. Our prayer is a participation in Christ's prayer and Christ's prayer is for the sustaining as well as for the completing of his kingdom.

and the dead being bound by a common hope for the resurrection of the body in the coming of the new creation. Three examples are worth noting. First, a text for use when the coffin is sprinkled with water:

> With this water we call to mind N's baptism.
> As Christ went through the deep waters of death for us,
> so may he bring N and all the redeemed
> to the fullness of the resurrection life.

Second, the collects (which are offered as alternatives):

> Merciful Father,
> hear our prayers and comfort us;
> renew our trust in your Son,
> whom you raised from the dead:
> strengthen our faith that N and
> all who have died in the love of Christ
> will share in his resurrection;
> who is alive and reigns with you,
> in the unity of the Holy Spirit,
> one God, now and for ever.

> Eternal God, our maker and redeemer,
> grant us, with N and all the faithful departed,
> the sure benefits of your Son's saving passion and
> glorious resurrection:
> that, in the last day, when you gather up all things in Christ,
> we may with them enjoy the fullness of your promises;
> through Jesus Christ your Son our Lord,
> who is alive and reigns with you,
> in the unity of the Holy Spirit,
> one God, now and for ever.

Third, a petition in the intercessions:

> Bring *him/her* and all who rest in Christ
> into the fullness of your kingdom
> where sins have been forgiven and death is no more.

None of these betrays the principles identified earlier. They do not undermine our assurance in the faithfulness of God's promises or our confidence that the dead are 'with the Lord,' but they do properly allow the church's traditional faith in the future completion of God's purposes to be turned into prayer. They are good ways of praying in relation to the departed.